How Much Does This Hold?

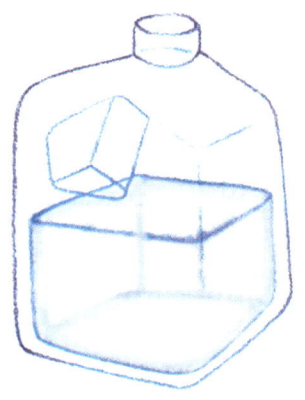

written by
Mia Coulton
illustrated by
Dennis Graves

Mom showed me how to measure using cups, pints, quarts and gallons. She used colored water.

She poured one cup of water into a one-pint jar.

The jar needed more water.

She poured another cup of water into the one-pint jar.

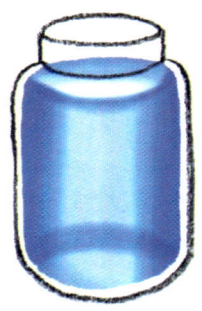

The jar was full!

Next Mom poured one pint of water into a one-quart pitcher.

The pitcher was not full.

She poured another pint of water into the one-quart pitcher.

The pitcher was full!

Mom let me pour one quart of water into a one-gallon jug.

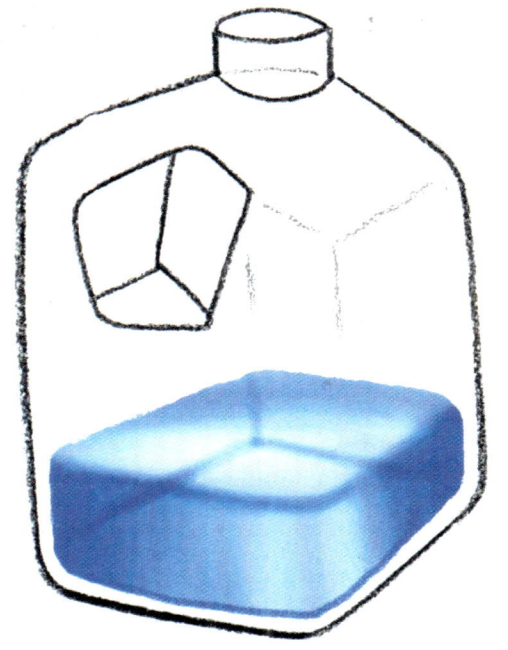

The jug was not full.

I poured another quart of water into the one-gallon jug.

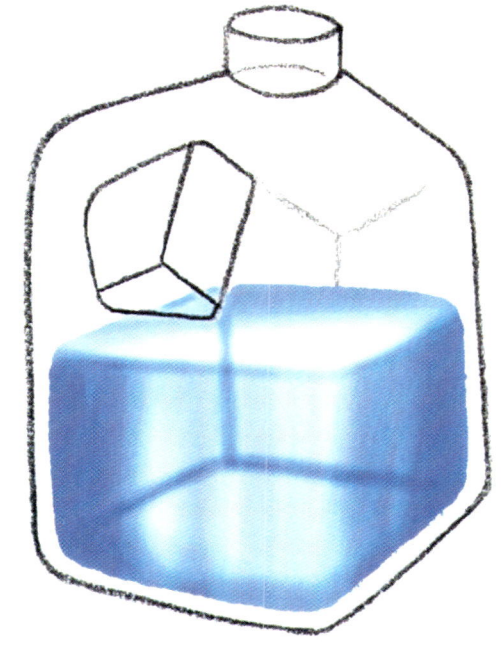

The jug was still not full.

I poured two more quarts of water into the one-gallon jug.

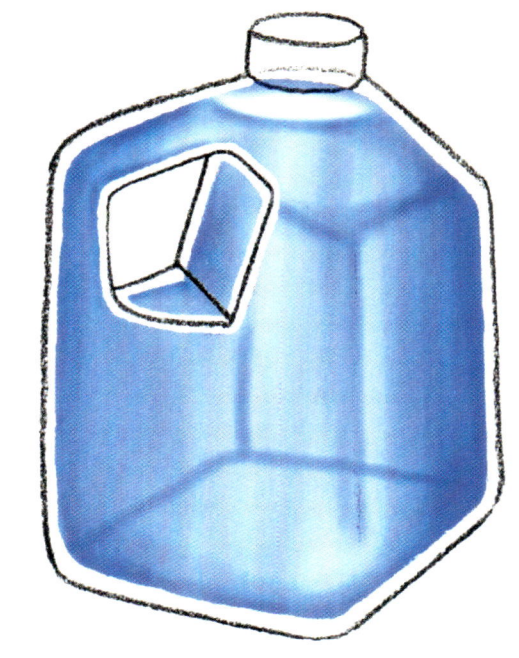

The jug was full!

Then I wanted to make some pink lemonade. I put some lemonade mix into a two-quart pitcher.

I poured water from a full one-gallon jug into the pitcher.

Some water was left in the one-gallon jug.

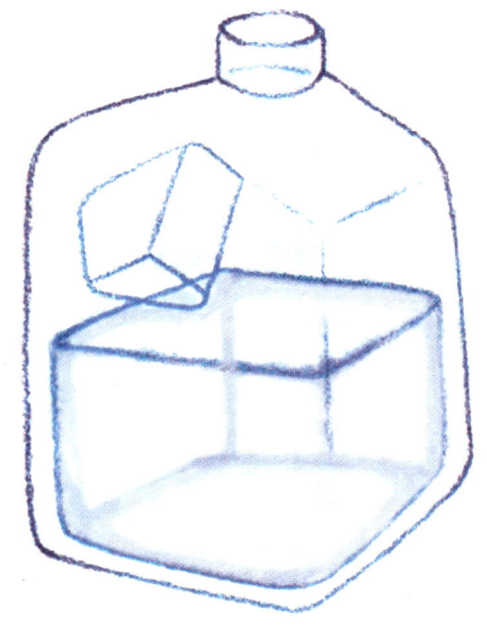

How much water was left in the one-gallon jug?